D0722793

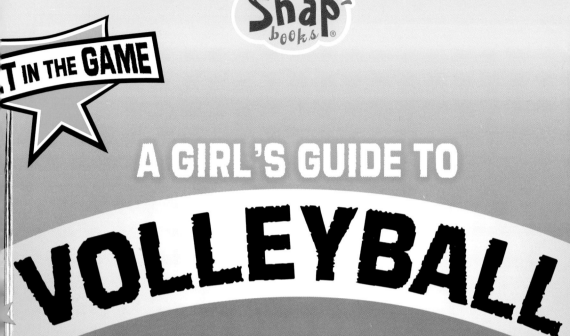

Snap books®

T IN THE GAME

A GIRL'S GUIDE TO
VOLLEYBALL

by Anastasia Suen

Consultant:
Peggy Miranda
Administrator, Louisiana Volleyball
AAU Volleyball Chair, Louisiana and Mississippi
Covington, Louisiana

Snap Books are published by Capstone Press,
1710 Roe Crest Drive, North Mankato, Minnesota 56003
www.capstonepub.com

Books published by Capstone Press are manufactured with paper
containing at least 10 percent post-consumer waste.

Library of Congress Cataloging-in-Publication Data
Suen, Anastasia.
  A girl's guide to volleyball / by Anastasia Suen.
      p. cm. — (Snap books. Get in the game.)
  Includes bibliographical references and index.
  Summary: "Quizzes, rules, and tips and tricks on how to play volleyball"—Provided by publisher.
  ISBN 978-1-4296-7673-1 (library binding)
  1. Volleyball for girls—Juvenile literature. I. Title.

  GV1015.4.W66S84 2012
  796.325082—dc23   2011036701

Editor: Mari Bolte
Designer: Bobbie Nuytten
Media Researcher: Eric Gohl
Production Specialist: Kathy McColley

Photo Credits:
Capstone Studio/Karon Dubke, 5, 6–7, 10, 12, 13 (court), 14 (bottom), 17, 20, 21, 23 (bottom),
25, 29; Getty Images/Washington Post/John McDonnell, cover (player); iStockphoto/
Christopher Futcher, 9; Newscom/Icon SMI 981/Alan Look, 15; Shutterstock/CREATISTA,
26 (bottom), Deklofenak, 27, Drozdowski, 19 (left), Hannamariah, 23 (top), hanzl, cover
(ball), back cover, 2, 4–5 (top), 7 (top right), 14 (top), 18 (top), 26 (top), Ildi Papp, 22, kanate,
8, mooinblack, 11, Roxanne McMillen, 16, sarsmis, 18 (bottom), Serg64, 19 (right), Terekhov
Igor, 13 (ball)

Design Elements
Shutterstock/Sergey Kandakov (stars); Solid (cheering crowd)

Printed in the United States of America in North Mankato, Minnesota.

102011   006405CGS12

TABLE OF CONTENTS

CHAPTER 1 ★

How Much Do You Know?

In 1895 coach William Morgan hung a tennis net high in the air. Then he gave his players a basketball. He told them to hit the ball over the net with their hands. Morgan called his new game mintonette. But that name didn't last long. The following year the name was changed to volleyball.

Today more than 800 million people worldwide sign up to show off their volleyball skills. They run, dive, jump, and hit the ball over thousands of nets around the world. Take the quiz to test your volleyball know-how!

1. How many players are allowed on each indoor team?
a) 6
b) 8
c) 10
d) 12

2. Before serving, a player must wait for:
a) the floor captain's nod
b) the coach's whistle
c) the referee's whistle
d) the crowd's cheers

3. How long does a game last?
a) 45 minutes
b) Until one team scores 25 points
c) Until a player is hurt
d) two 15-minute quarters

4. If a team doesn't serve in the order shown in the lineup card, they:

a) get to start over

b) lose the serve

c) lose the points

d) lose the serve and, in some cases, points

5. Which of these is true?

a) After the serve, the other team can touch the ball six times in a row.

b) After the serve, the serving team can touch the ball immediately.

c) After the serve, the other team can touch the ball three times in a row.

d) After the serve, the other team automatically scores a point.

6. Which move is illegal contact with the ball?

a) catching the ball

b) passing the ball

c) blocking the ball

d) bumping the ball

7. Spiking is hitting the ball with what body part?

a) head

b) both hands

c) one hand

d) forearms

8. A block happens:

a) above the net

b) on the net

c) in the middle of the net

d) below the net

9. To dig the ball, a player scoops it with:

a) her fingers or wrists

b) her hands or forearms

c) her head

d) her shoulder

10. If a ball is very close to the ground after being hit, a player can:

a) rest

b) crash

c) roll

d) serve

answers at the bottom of page 31

CHAPTER 2 ★

The Basics

Working the Offense

Girls play tough, and nobody plays tougher than volleyball girls. In volleyball you get to play every position. As the game goes on, players move clockwise around the court. Each girl gets to serve, play back and front court, and be on offense and defense. Some players specialize in front row or back row positions.

The number of players on each team depends on where the game is played. If you are playing on the beach, a team of two will do. Indoor games are played with six girls who love to **spike** the ball.

You won the coin toss, so your team gets to serve the ball. The server stands anywhere along the end line. When the referee blows the whistle, the server tosses the ball into the air. She uses an overhand serve for more power and accuracy. With her palm to the floor, she swings her arm and sends the ball over the net. Now it's up to the other team to return the ball. The players on the other team cannot slow down the ball by catching it.

SPIKE: a forceful hit made by a player to gain a point

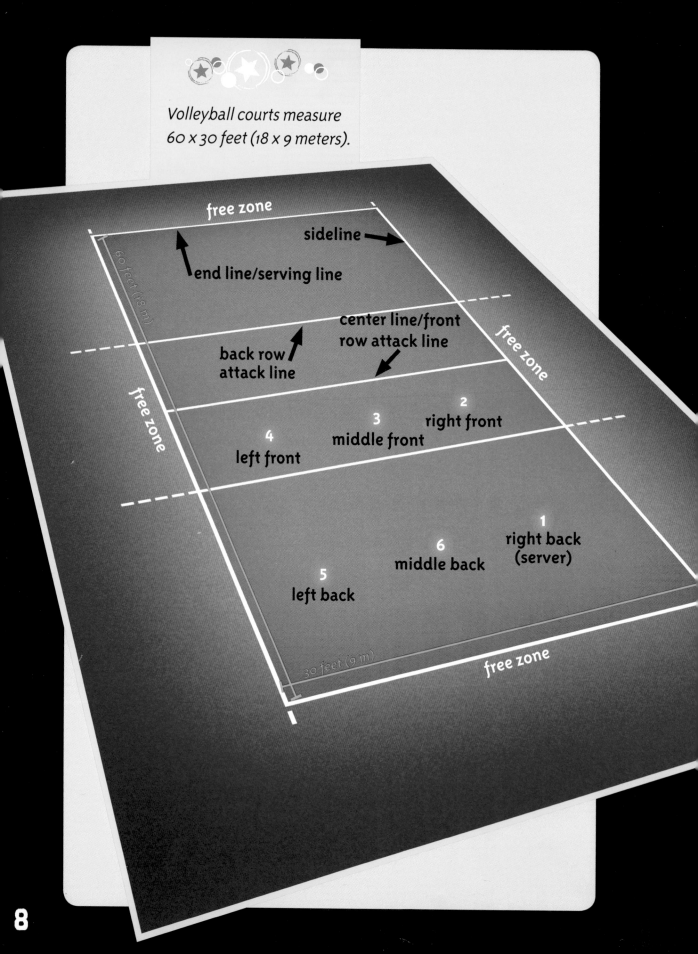

Volleyball courts measure 60 x 30 feet (18 x 9 meters).

free zone

sideline

end line/serving line

60 feet (18 m)

center line/front row attack line

back row attack line

free zone

free zone

2
right front

3
middle front

4
left front

1
right back
(server)

6
middle back

5
left back

30 feet (9 m)

free zone

8

The other team must return the ball before it hits the ground. If the ball hits the ground after a serve, the serving team scores a point. Each team can only touch the ball three times in a row. The only exception is when a player touches the ball to block. After the block, the ball can still be touched three more times by that player's team.

Most teams handle the ball with a pass-set-spike play. The first player passes the ball. The forward pass is often used here. The player stands with her feet shoulder-width apart. Her hands are together, and her thumbs are facing up. She uses her forearms to pass the ball to another player on her team.

The second player **sets** the ball. She moves her hands above her head and keeps her fingers wide apart. She uses her fingertips to send to the ball to another player. That sets up the third and final shot.

This third shot is the spike. The player times her jump to hit the ball when the ball is at the highest point. She hits the ball with the palm of her hand and snaps her wrist. She sends the ball straight down on the other side of the net. If everything goes right, the ball should hit the floor, earning her team a point. But if the player on the other team blocks the spike, the ball stays in the air and the game continues.

ET: using the fingertips
direct the ball to a player
o can spike it across the net

Games are split into periods called sets. Two out of three sets must be won in junior varsity games. The regular sets are played to 25 points. If each team has won a set each, the third set is the tiebreaker. Varsity games are similar, except five sets are played instead of three. Regular sets end when one team scores 15 points. Tiebreaker sets are played to 25 points. In all sets, the winning team also must lead by two points. So if the score is 15 to 14, the leading team needs to score another point to win.

Let's Hear It for Defense!

The other team returns the ball to your side of the court. The players in the front row jump up and block the ball. They can use both hands to hit the ball. However, touching the top of the net while blocking is illegal.

If the ball gets past the front row, it's up to a player in the back to keep the ball moving. If you're playing in the back row, get ready to dig! The technique for digging is similar to passing. Stand with your feet apart and crouch down. Keep your weight forward. Put your hands together with your thumbs on top so the ball bounces off your forearms. The idea is to pop the ball into the air and set your teammate up for an easy shot.

There are five emergency plays that a player can use if the ball is about to hit the ground. The first three are the collapse, sprawl, or dive. The only difference between the three is how much your body moves. When a player collapses, she simply falls to the ground to reach the ball. A sprawl involves taking a step before hitting the ground. Diving is similar to the sprawl, but the player is more airborne.

Rolling will get a player back into the game quickly. After hitting the ball, the player uses her forward movement to roll to her feet.

A final defensive technique is called the pancake. It's a lot like the sprawl. Instead of bumping the ball with her arms, the player's hand is spread flat on the ground. The ball bounces off the back of her hand.

For all these techniques, it's important to keep your weight forward and be on your toes. Keep your body close to the ground to avoid injury.

Out of Bounds?

Getting the ball over the net for a serve is important. Pay attention to where the ball lands after a hit. If the ball goes out of bounds, it's considered a fault, and the other team gets a point. If your team was serving the ball, they also lose the serve.

What is out of bounds? The most basic out-of-bounds fault occurs when the ball lands outside the court. But what happens if the ball touches something on the way over? That usually means the ball is out of bounds too. If the ball hits the antenna on the net, it is out of bounds. The ball has to cross over the net without touching any part of it. The referee's platform is also out of bounds.

If the ball hits the ceiling and then goes over the net, that is also considered out of bounds. The only exception is if the ball hits the ceiling on your side. If the ball comes back down, you can keep the ball in play.

CHAPTER 3 ★

Staying Fit to Win

Volleyball requires teamwork, quick thinking, and fast movements. All of this work benefits your body. You'll use muscles in both your upper and lower body. Your hand, arm, and shoulder muscles get a good workout when you serve and pass. And chasing the ball works your lower body. Your hips, thighs, quads, and hamstrings will get stronger and faster.

Keeping your body fit will improve your game. Not only will you find it easier to learn new moves, you'll also be able to play for longer periods. A healthy body is key to playing your best game.

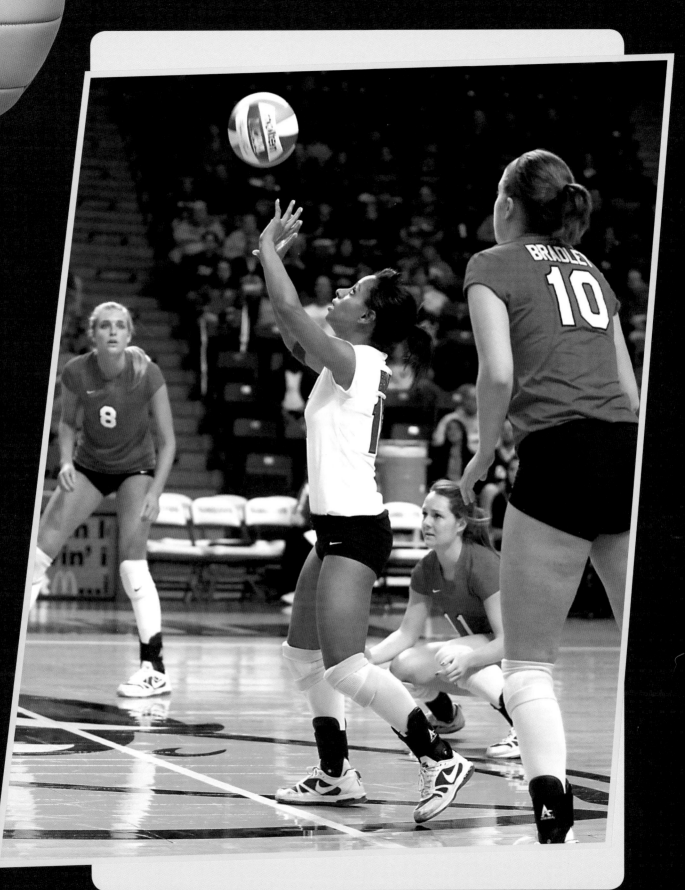

Focusing on Safety

Like any sport, volleyball has its risks. Play it safe. Wear comfortable shoes designed for the volleyball court. Good support inside the shoe will protect your knees and ankles from injury. And make sure your shoes have good soles. You'll want to move around the court easily and without slipping.

Keep your knees safe by wearing knee pads. Playing volleyball puts a lot of stress on the **ligaments** that help the knee pivot and turn. Girls are two to eight times more likely than boys to injure their knees. The female body produces the hormone **estrogen**. This hormone weakens the body's ligaments, making injury more likely.

If you are playing beach volleyball, good sunglasses are a must! Wear sunscreen and lip balm too. A hat helps block the sun.

Be sure to stretch well before and after the game. Stretching will get your blood flowing to your muscles. Blood will give your muscles the nourishment they need. Stretching also helps minimize injury.

A healthy body is important to staying safe. Many schools and organizations require a physical every year, so see a doctor before the season starts. He or she will make sure your body is running right. Keep your body in top shape, even in the off-season. Try strength-building exercises, such as squats or push-ups. Workouts that focus on strengthening your core muscles, such as sit-ups and stability ball exercises, will also help your lower back. This training will make you more flexible, which is a valuable skill for a volleyball player.

Finally, make sure you get plenty of rest the night before the game. A player who is tired or overworked is more likely to suffer an injury.

CHAPTER 4 ★

Eat Right, Play Right

Food is fuel. That's a fact. You need food to keep your body moving. Food gives you the energy you need to keep playing.

Your body takes the food you eat and turns it into energy. Complex **carbohydrates**, such as pasta, cereal, or rice keep your body going. Complex carbs are also found in fresh veggies, fruit, and dairy products. But steer clear of simple carbs like those found in fast food. Your body digests simple carbs right away. Complex carbs are digested slowly and give your body more long-lasting energy. That means you'll have enough pep to get through rally after rally.

CARBOHYDRATE: a substance that gives you energy

Easy-to-Eat Complex Carbs		
dairy	• low-fat milk • yogurt	• cheese
fruits	• apricots • grapes • plums	• bananas • apples
vegetables	• broccoli • spinich • eggplant	• celery • carrots • greens
legumes	• lentils • chickpeas	• black beans • peas
whole grains	• brown or wild rice • whole grain bread • pasta	• oats • cereal

Tip: Your body needs a variety of foods to perform its best. Don't forget to add protein, calcium, vitamins, minerals, and even fats to your daily diet.

Staying Hydrated

Playing gets your body moving, and an active body gets hot! And when you're hot, you sweat. Sweating is how your body cools itself. It's important to stay hydrated, so drink lots of fluids before, during, and after the game. Water and sports drinks can keep your body working well.

Your body is 75 percent water. As you sweat, your body loses water. If you don't replace lost fluids, you may become **dehydrated**. Dehydration can cause headaches and fatigue. Some people get upset or restless. Others become confused.

Dehydration affects the rest of your body too. It can make your muscles cramp up or ache. Your skin may be covered with sweat. Instead of feeling hot, you'll feel cold and clammy. And you may get an upset stomach. These are all symptoms of **heatstroke**. Tell your coach, and then grab something to drink and go somewhere cool.

DEHYDRATION: a medical condition caused by a lack of water

HEATSTROKE: a serious illness caused by working in the heat too lo

Don't Forget about Fluids!	
2 hours before working out:	8–16 ounces (240–480 milliliters) of water
30 minutes before working out:	8–16 ounces of water
15 minutes after you start your workout:	3–6 ounces (90–180 mL) of water
30 minutes after you start your workout:	3–6 ounces of water
45 minutes after you start your workout:	3–6 ounces of water
after working out:	8–16 ounces of water for every pound you have lost while working out

Refueling After the Game

You need to feed your body after a hard workout. All the carbohydrates your body used up need to be replaced. Dig in to big bowls of brown rice, quinoa, fruits, and vegetables. These complex carbs will help your body feel refreshed. Your tired muscles will also need protein, which help your muscles repair themselves. Stick with lean or low-fat proteins, such as beans and peas, nuts and seeds, seafood, and lean cuts of beef, pork, and chicken.

Tip: Be sure the amount of protein you eat falls within the USDA's MyPlate serving size recommendation. Girls between the ages of 9 and 18 should have 5 ounces (142 grams) of protein a day.

You'll also need to replace your body's **electrolytes**. Your body needs these minerals to work properly. Some foods with natural electrolytes include fruit juices, coconut water, milk, fruits, and vegetables. Sports drinks are full of electrolytes that will get your body rehydrated. But don't overdo it—sports drinks can be full of empty calories too. Instead, sip water or eat watery fruit, such as grapes or watermelon. And avoid grabbing a soda. The carbonation will trick your body into thinking you've had enough to drink.

ECTROLYTE: a mineral that
ries electricity in your body so you
think and move

Tip: You may be surprised to hear that a glass of chocolate milk is a great post-game drink. It's the perfect mixture of carbs, protein, and fat to help your body resupply itself. Make milk moustaches cool again!

LAYERED BANANABERRY SMOOTHIE ★

Looking for something tasty to eat after the big game? Try this smoothie! This cool treat will refresh you, nourish your skin, and help your body bounce back from hard work. Choose a yogurt flavor that will complement your berry selection. Vanilla, honey, or mixed berry are good choices.

INGREDIENTS

1 cup (240 milliliters) vanilla yogurt
1 ½ cup (360 mL) milk
½ cup (120 mL) ice cubes
½ small banana

¾ cup (175 mL) blueberries
    or strawberries (fresh or frozen)
granola or diced fruit

TOOLS

liquid measuring cup
blender

small bowl
drinking glass

Step 1: Divide yogurt, milk, and ice cubes into two portions. Place one portion of each ingredient in the blender. Add banana. Blend until smooth.

Step 2: Pour mixture into the bowl and set aside.

Step 3: Add berries and the second portion of yogurt, milk, and ice to the blender. Blend until smooth.

Step 4: Alternate layering the two mixtures in the drinking glass.

Step 5: Top with granola or fruit.

Tip: Pour the smoothie mixtures slowly over the back of a spoon while layering. Pouring this way will help keep the layers separate.

More Berry Delights

There are many ways to make a smoothie. Try different berries, such as raspberries or blackberries. Shake it up by using more than one kind of berry. Make it dairy-free by using silken tofu instead of yogurt. Change the flavor by using orange juice or lemonade instead of milk. Experiment and enjoy!

CHAPTER 5 ★

Girls Just Wanna Have Fun

All work and no play is no fun. Get your teammates together after the game and share a bonding experience! Try a girl's night in. Pop a healthy pizza into the oven and give yourselves makeovers. Watch your favorite chick flick. Have a karaoke night and sing and dance along with your favorite concert or TV show.

Keep your team spirit going even after volleyball season is over. Grab your girls and go for a run. Join a gym and set up a weekly workout schedule. Cross-train together and form a soccer or softball team. The more time you spend together off-court, the better your teamwork will be on-court!

You need the whole team playing together to win. Volleyball teaches you how to communicate with your team members. By trusting your teammates to do their part, you're sure to play your best.

Yoga is just one way to bond with your teammates.

NO-SEW BANDANA TOTE BAG ★

You won't need a sewing machine to make this cute bandana tote! Use it to carry your gear to every game.

WHAT YOU'LL NEED:

iron
two 22-inch (56-centimeter) square bandanas

fabric scissors
ruler or measuring tape
straight pins

Step 1: Have an adult iron the bandanas.

Step 2: Cut a 1-inch (2.5-cm) border off one bandana. Start at one corner, and cut all the way around the bandana so the border is in one long strip. Repeat with the second bandana. Set the fabric strips aside.

Step 3: Lay the bandanas together with the wrong sides touching each other. Pin the bandanas together.

Step 4: Make a 3-inch (7.6-cm) cut along one edge of the bandanas. Continue making fringe cuts all the way around the bandanas. The cuts should be spaced ¾-inch (1.9-cm) apart.

Step 5: Cut off the squares at each corner of the bandanas and discard.

Step 6: Tie the fringe strips to each other in double knots. Continue knotting until three sides of the bag are tied. Remove straight pins.

Step 7: Cut each of the border scraps in half to make four long strips of fabric.

Step 8: Braid three of the strips together. Make a knot at each end of the braid.

Step 9: Tie the ends of the strips to the bag to make a handle.

Step 10: With an adult's help, iron the top fringe so it lays flat.

Tip: Can't find a bandana you like? Use fabric squares that are 22 inches (.61 yards) long on all sides.

GLOSSARY

carbohydrate (kar-boh-HYE-drate)—a substance found in foods such as bread, rice, cereal, and potatoes that gives you energy

dehydration (dee-hy-DRAY-shuhn)—a life-threatening medical condition caused by a lack of water

electrolyte (ih-LEK-truh-lahyt)—a mineral that encourages the body to drink more water; electrolytes contain an electric charge

estrogen (es-TRUH-juhn)—a hormone produced only by females

heatstroke (HEET-strohk)—a serious illness caused by working in the heat too long

ligament (lig-UH-mehnt)—a band of tissue that connects or supports bones and joints

set (SET)—using the fingertips to direct the ball to a player who can spike it across the net

spike (SPIKE)—a forceful hit made by a player to gain a point; a spike is also called a bury, hammer, or kill

READ MORE

Crossingham, John. *Spike it Volleyball*. Sports Starters. New York: Crabtree Pub. Co., 2008.

Evdokimoff, Natasha. *Volleyball: In the Zone*. New York: AV2 by Weigl, 2011.

McDougall, Chros. *Girls Play to Win Volleyball*. Girls Play to Win. Chicago: Norwood House Press, 2011.

INTERNET SITES

FactHound offers a safe, fun way to find Internet sites related to this book. All of the sites on FactHound have been researched by our staff.

Here's all you do:

Visit *www.facthound.com*

Type in this code: 9781429676731

Check out projects, games and lots more at
www.capstonekids.com

QUIZ ANSWERS: 1. a 2. c 3. b 4. d 5. c 6. a 7. c 8. a 9. b 10. c

INDEX